INTIMATIONS

For Betty

Against all Odds,
As Usual
You prevailed.
Welcome from us all

Mike

INTIMATIONS

POEMS 2002 - 2005

MIKE O'BRIEN

PUBLISHED BY
TWO OAKS

Published in 2006 by Two Oaks
27 Westhawe, Peterborough
PE3 8BA

© Mike O'Brien 2005

All rights reserved. No part of this publication
may be reproduced, stored in or introduced into
a retrieval system, or transmitted by any means
without prior permission of the copyright owner.

ISBN 978-0-9551620-0-8

Distributed by Two Oaks
27 Westhawe, Peterborough
PE3 8BA

For my wife Maggie and for my children
and grandchildren who in their various
ways made this slim volume necessary.

Also:

Two poems 'The Brotherhood' and 'St. Joseph's a Remembrance' are dedicated to those who endured the hardship and the inhumanity of a Dickensian institution between the wars and survived to enjoy the liberation of a Salesian College.

ACKNOWLEDGEMENTS

Several of these poems first appeared in anthologies published by *Poetry Now* and *Dogma Publications*.

INTRODUCTION

While most of these poems deal with readily identifiable subjects there are two that need some explanation. Entitled "The Brotherhood" and "St. Joseph's" they describe the harsh years spent by a few hundred boys in the care of a well meaning, but woefully ill trained, religious order. We were, in general, exposed to this authoritarian regime from the age of four to fourteen, during the 1930s to the late 1940s. For many of us it was characterised by physical abuse, harsh discipline and disgusting food, for nine years. Release came for the lucky few who were sent to a Salesian College in Gloucestershire. The contrast was so vivid that 70 years later many of us return to the village and its surroundings every year. These two poems put on record my take on the Purgatory and the subsequent comparative Paradise visited upon us in our years of innocence.

For the rest, the poems on offer here reflect a side of me that I doubt my family or friends realised existed. It has been a surprise to me also.
Mike O'B

CONTENTS

The Hands that Fused the Force	1
Glimpses	2
Abandoned	3
The River Runs Over my Bones	4
Chaos	5
Once Upon a Time	6
False Dawn	8
In Sligo	9
On Marcle Ridge	10
Day One in the Factory	11
Making a Call from Ireland	12
Sunset	14
Intimations	15
The Grebe	16

I Remember Charlie	17
The Ploughing Team	18
Softly is the Hill	21
Listen You!	22
OCH!	23
Summer Idyll	24
The Immigrant	26
The Stag	28
A Passing	29
Fugue	30
The Rain	32
St. Joseph's a Remembrance	33
The Brotherhood	36
A visit to . . .	40
Nightfall	42
Notes	46

The Hands that Fused the Force that Pulled the Lever

Whose hands were they that fused the force
That shook the river's bed to change its course,
That purged the plain and barren made
The mountain range and woodland glade?

Whose hands were they that pulled the lever
And released the virus of the must-have fever,
That spilled the blood and broke the brow
Of the half a billion starving now?

Whose grasping hands will fail to connect
The avaricious cause to its beggaring effect?
Who cares? It seems to matter less not more
When hunger reigns on a distant shore.

Glimpses

The shadow falls from the tree
And lays, slowly moving,
Avoiding the sun, fearing exposure
Will put an end to its
Thin ethereality.

Sharp edged clarity of the secret
Truth of things comes fleetingly.
Too searching an effort
And the substance fades.

Trust, and a glimpse is born
But cannot be grasped and
Brought to light in the common day,
For like a dying shadow
It will fade and slip away.

Abandoned

The Child spoke,
"It's not my mum
That figure on the bed.
My mum was full, not empty.
My mum was lively,
She was not still like that.
How can it be?
She would never leave me!
She talked.
She sang
Did my mum".

The figure on the bed did not stir
Neither did it smile
Or sing.
The face was vacant,
The hair unkempt.
The love once there
Away in the stars.

Maybe it is there I must go
Thought the child.

If my hair was unkempt
And my brow pale
And a stillness descended upon me,
Then I could take that journey
And sing again.

The River Runs Over My Bones

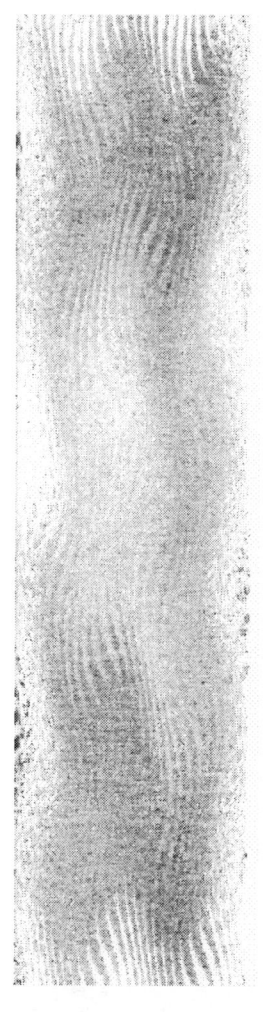

The river runs over my bones

While I sit on the bank alone.

The song will go on

'Til the last bone's gone

While the river runs over my bones.

The river runs over my bones

And it's taking my mind away.

Will nothing stop its downhill run

And my skull from echoing its song

While the river runs over my bones?

O the river runs over my bones

As it did at the first light of day

But the cataract's fall at the rocky leap

And the whirling pool where waters deep

Are threatening to wash them away.

Chaos

I have a sensitive dependence
On initial conditions
As they say.
I wonder, will I
Be depressed,
Visionary
Or inspired
Today.
Or not?
Those butterflies
Clapping their wings
Carelessly;
Just another clap
Might have made a difference
To my day,
Or
Perhaps there was a clap
Too many.
Sometimes I wonder
Why I am sensitive dependant
And then
I wonder why
I wonder why?
Those butterflies ?..............

Once Upon a Time

With arrows and spears from distant lands,
Plundering and pillaging,
On the hunt for spoils,
Came the Neolithic marauding bands.

Setting the standard of human behaviour,
Taking and destroying,
Establishing a norm
A path to follow, a future cynosure.

Then came the Bronze Age and a new artisan.
O! new tools for felling
And new tools for killing
And new weapon dealers for the old partisan.

The plundering and pillaging grew ever wilder;
Pressure for land,
A need for stock
And for meat to take home to the childer.

The plundering had begun with hardly a whisper.
But hey! they found gold;
And then they found silver,
and tin,
and lead,
and iron,
and coal,
and copper.

Then came aluminium
And then the minerals
Ad infinitum
Except……
There was a limit but we plundered on.
Learning to pollute,
Blinded by tyranny
Of the growth god, partnered by mammon.

With no will to restore a balance,
Swirling heat
Stifled the planet.
We'd never given the future a glance.

Homo Sapiens with all of their skill
Struggled, unable
To shut Pandora's box,
So now were just grist to nature's mill.

When an asteroid swept in from the sky
With an Almighty blast
And purgatorial fire,
The end of the world was truly nigh.

But there was nobody, but nobody,
To hear,
Or rue,
Or even acknowledge the distant passing
Of a hominid species, long, long gone.

False Dawn

Faint glow glancing,
Feather-touching the sky,
Lighting the way for Helios
To ride his chariot by.

Such high flown promises
For yet another day,
Of help to the multitude
But will they have a say?

Hear their hollow laughter
At our widespread obesity,
Unknown in hunger's lexicon
Now a growing obscenity.

While Helios rides in the East
And the sun follows his path,
Will the Haves continue to feast
While Have-Nots are eaten by wrath?

In Sligo

Into the corner arrive
four portly men and bald
bringing conviviality,
snug as Merino wool.

Their bubble of words
and comfortable laughter
drift out and around
invading the quietude.

I emerge from my shell
and, raised in spirit, send
four glasses of Chablis
with nodding smile.

But a silence intrudes.
Glasses are raised
Tho' the pebble thrown
disturbs the portly pool.

Now good manners
and curiosity reign.
Mute regrets colour my replies,
as I reach to disconnect

while parrying their flow;
eager that they resume
their private conviviality
and me return to isolation.

Laughter and fellowship
echo as I leave, confirming
that here, I am a stranger
waiting for the train.

On Marcle Ridge

Public footpath the signpost read.
I slipped through the leaning gate,
Sweeping meadows met the eye
But just inside and to the left
Sat a carvéd seat of stone,
It read:

"Placed here by her six children as she loved this place and they loved her"

Compelled I sat.
                      Across a majestic landscape
                      Of wooded hills and green fields rolling,
                      Rages the wind, keening out of the West
                      At the loss of such a lover.
                      Stolid oaks and gallant beech sway in consolation
                      While the toy tractor below busies itself
                      With other things self-importantly.
                      The serried clouds queuing in the West
                      Await their turn to cast acknowledgement,
                      Fleeting their shadows o'er the memorial stone.
                      High above mewing buzzards mourn the loss
                      But the sun shines with never ending zest
                      Upon this Eden where her memory rests.

Day One in the Factory

In the pavilions of the grey machines
My senses are seized,
Whirled, and spun about
By black-white news in a palsied grip.
From the clanking, spinning
Perpetually repeated
The mind becomes a wound.
Oh blood!
A gaping oozing maw.

I do not like those grey machines.
But the men? the women?
Were they dignified – once?
And full of hope – once?
Hurry up
I will not march,
I cannot march
To the drum,
To the endless hum
Of those grey machines.

Unbind my aching brow
And let pour slowly,
Thickening on to the gritty street,
Deadening the peak-capped voice,
My blood!
Then lead me to the viscous tar
And daub and seal.
But hurt no more
This country mind.

Making a Call from Ireland

(With acknowledgement to Henry Reed)

Today is the day for ringing your wife,
Yesterday you saw the megaliths
And tomorrow it's the music festival
But today is the day for ringing your wife.

Yesterday you bought a telephone card
Upon which are the dialling instructions.
First choose one of the ten digit codes
One of which will probably work.

Next you will pick up the receiver
And dial that ten-digit code.
A voice will ask for the pin number
Printed faintly on the telephone card.

Now never let anyone see you
Entering the twelve-digit number;
For this you will need a third hand,
Which in your case you have not got.

So place the receiver between your knees
But don't let the bleeder hang,
Now a distant voice is repeating,
"Enter the number you wish to call".

The voice will be insistent,
It wants the number you're trying to call,
Remember to add the local four digits
Making thirty-six digits in all.

With luck your number will be ringing
And your wife will pick up the call.
You will hear her clearly speaking
Though she will not hear you at all.

You think you have made a hash
Of trying to ring your wife
But your telephone card has the answer
At the bottom in very small print:

"If you wish to make a follow-up call
Place your finger on the button marked hash
Carefully press the hash button twice"
Which, when you do, cuts off your wife.

Outside a blackbird is singing,
To her mate in a nearby tree,
His answer is clear and ringing
And their songs sweep away o'er the lea.

*****

SUNSET

The sun an eyeless socket staring
In the weak of sky vein-blue
Is bleeding cold blood.

In the stumbling half-light
The shadows thicken
And tumble distorted.

Softly over the hushed grass
Creeps the dying day wind
And the damp leaves shiver.

The red-sore rim drops slowly,
Slowly dropping amid purple
Sprung hills stretching softly

With sweet yearning, to envelop
Deeply, the whole sun completely,
And so give birth to the night.

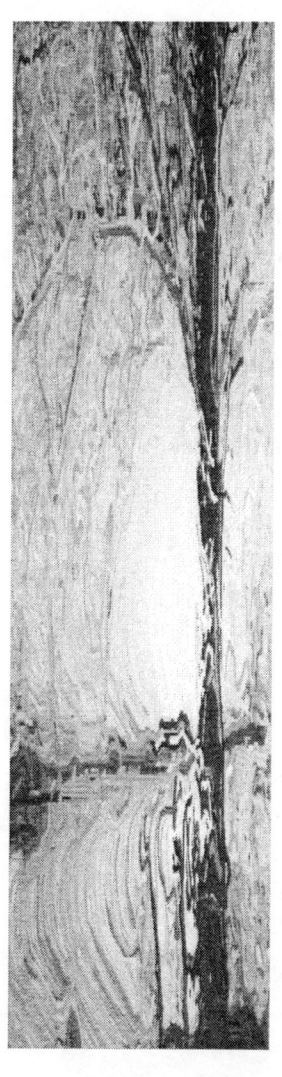

INTIMATIONS

The evening's golden West

Sets the lake on fire

While the sky maintains a blue

Of aching delicacy.

Lines of gold shimmer

Across the lake following

As I move around its edge.

A smudge of cloud of purest white

Sits above in transit

To the coming night.

Trees stand around unaware

But even as my spirit lifts

A pang emerges of regret.

The trees, the sky, the hedges,

Flaunt their permanence

With each Season's passing,

Unaware, always unaware.

But I'll be gone and they still there.

The Grebe
(For Kate)

Stiff necked, crested and shy
He will not look you in the eye
But dive until he thinks you've gone
And surface when he's good and done
Those things that Grebes do under water
That take inordinate time and laughter.
And that is why
He will not look you in the eye.
Try guessing where he'll surface next
If you want to see him vexed.
But please don't look at him askance
Unless you want to see him dance.
A Grebe when dancing needs a mate
So be prepared to make a date
But never stare – a big mistake
Or at the bottom of the lake
You'll find the secret of their laughter.
The Grebes are doing what Grebes oughter
Burying nosey parkers under water.

I Remember Charlie

Sometimes we found him, smiling goofily
but still in the saddle,
bike and Charlie leaning crazily in the hedge
while the measures of rough cider
worked their merriment.

Hedges he laid with a craftsman's hand
his billhook flashing
as the blackthorn was cut and forcefully bent.
Buds bursting white the following spring, transforming
the hedge to a snowy tapestry.

Whenever we met his greeting would be,
How bist? our cheeky reply, how bist thee?

His was a West Glo'shire accent

rising deep in his throat, dwelling awhile,

then delivered with a generous plume of spittle.

Life had not festooned him with gifts,
just his clothes and a bike.
Young, we had our lives spread before us,

Ageing, dark death lay waiting for him.
For this oak of a man carried a fear of the workhouse.

When age and work had wearied him,
dignity was denied.
To the workhouse he went, in the workhouse he died.

But the farm boys at Blaisdon in the '40's
still fondly recall Charlie,
Hedger, Ditcher, true Son of the Soil
of Blaisdon, Glo'shire.

The Ploughing Team

Sam the Shire horse met the morning air
Already harnessed for the plough,
And turned to look for his ploughing mate
Bonny the young grey Percheron mare.

Led by the bridle their harnesses creaking
They walked in unison,
Casting long shadows in the early sun,
Stopping where the plough lay resting.

The night's autumnal dew had laid a light kiss
Of rust on the mouldboard.
Bonny and Sam were hooked up
To the swing-trees lying in the wet grass.

The traces stretch under the strain,
As Bonny and Sam take the call
And the plough comes around on its heel
Leaving an imprint where it had lain.

With Bonny in the furrow and Sam on the land,
Taut traces and a hissing ploughshare,
Smoothed the soil along the mouldboard
Turning a furrow 'neath the ploughman's hand.

As the plough, the horses, the man and the soil
Were conjoined in a unit of one,
The ploughman sang his song of the earth
With music that came from his toil.

As they ploughed the organic connection grew,
Horses, ploughman, soil and plough,
Re-connecting with a distant voice,
Now once more being heard anew.

The only reality for the team that day
Was the warming sun, the hissing share,
The horses relentless pull 'til noon
Then time for oats, nosebag and hay.

While horses rested the ploughman ate,
Quietly surveying the furrows turned.
A craftsman's pride took hold
And he knew they'd plough 'til late.

Up and down the lea the furrows fell,
Straight as a die and uniform.
The horses did not seem to tire,
The ploughman caught in its spell.

He followed the pull of Gelding and Mare
The Coulter's unerring cut,
The Mouldboard's irresistible thrust
And the endless swish of soil over Share.

When dusk came creeping from the woods
And lent its chilling touch
To quieten the hedgerow's chatter
Of Chaffinch, Robin and Sparrow broods,

It was time to halt the pulling pair.
Time to loosen the traces,
Time to unhook the swing-trees
And leave the plough leaning there.

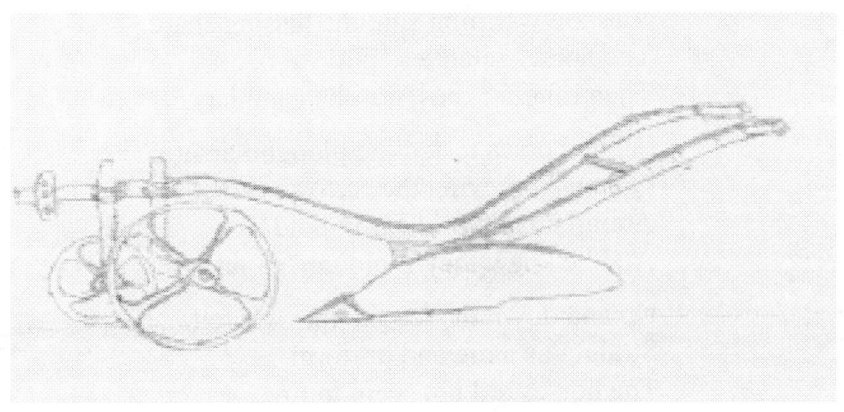

Softly is the Hill

Softly is the hill as it tends my inclination
As step by step fleet time steals my stay.
Crisp leaved Beech whisper their consternation,
But the distant horizon is where my thoughts lay.

Steam rose in clouds under Winter's grey
As the meadow fell to the old iron plough,
Just me and the horses we filled the day
And the rhythm we made is what I miss now.

Sam the Shire and Bonny the grey
Seemed as organic as the lea I once trod.
But now I'm an alien and lost in my way,
Together no longer we turn no clay sod.

The hill understands as I gaze to the West,
The Glo'shire meadows hold me in sway.
Faraway memories will not let me rest
And hearing their call I know I can't stay.

Listen You!

Remember youth the years,
Indulge your folly now.
Shock the settled way,
Gasp-make the city sheep.

Baa! Baa!
They flock in wonderment.
Look! their gaping jaws
Uplifted bleat.

While youth, finger raised
In pointed scorn,
Taunt with derisive laughter,
"We, we are the strong".

But dim, with tired feet stumbling
Resentfully, they join the sheep
Who towards tomorrow slowly go
And watch amazed the youth cavort.

OCH!

The Scotsman,
He speaks so fast.
I listen.
My ears rattle
With the word song.
New compounds
Some compressed,
Some stretched
With corners knocked off.
Emerging in a jetstream
From a bag of a mouth,
Falling through the air,
Foreign to my ear,
A new music
Fragmented and angular.

Summer Idyll

The Nene's grassy bank basks under the sun,
The boys spread themselves out to bathe,
Around them bicycles carelessly lay,
While the river thro' the reeds makes its run.

No worries carried to sully their pleasure
Left behind in the grey world of town,
Just their friends and the afternoon sun
As they laze in the grass by the river.

The skylark fills the air with its song
As Icarus-like it heads for the sun.
A Kestrel swooping by on the wing
Casts its shadow o'er skylark's young.

Five horses stand on the bend in the river
Heads drooping with sorrowful eyes,
Fighting the torment of the humbling flies
With a toss of the head and a skin shaking shiver.

Too hot for reeds to do more than rustle
In a shuffling conspiratorial whisper,
Audible only to the single reed warbler
Who decides to forego its habitual bustle.

Drifting slowly thro' the sky blue air
An aeroplane lazily drones,
While the boys splash about in the river
In a world of their own without care.

*****

The Immigrant

I saw a man.
He carried dignity
as an African tribeswoman
might carry water.

His clothes hung
on a slender frame.
Hair was white with wisdom;
long thin hands.

He turned them
as he explained
to the doctor of medicine,
the little problem

In a patient way;
both hands raised
and then a courteous descent
palms facing down.

His quiet words,
regal emphasis
Crowning his broken English
with gracious nod.

Backing away,
zipping his jacket,
squaring his shoulders, turning
his collar down,

Towards the exit
he made his way.
Lifting his head to face a mob
he stepped outside.

The police station
backyard was empty.
A smoker puffed his ten o'clock fag.
A bike lay on its side.

This was his new dominion.

*****

The Stag

The eye of the Stag
Coursed over me.
Wind and rain
Lashed the leaves
From the autumn oak.

Imperious and threatening,
Part tree, part animal,
Nevertheless vulnerable
With lofty arrogance,
Poised in the gloom.

An ancient clash;
While leaves and wind
Rattled and sang,
I was the hunter
And could not move.

I held its eye,
We neither blinked
And connection trembled
As understanding
Hovered between us.

I raised my pen,
He shook his head
And turned away.

A Passing

On a damp autumnal evening
When fog swathes the street
The road black and glistening
Writhes under careless feet.

Once gay leaves that danced
At every chattering gust
Now lay where the sun once glanced
Quietly turning into dust.

FUGUE
(After a brush with a bureaucrat in the Reference Library)

He sat there
Looking smug and smiling.
His glasses reflect his power
To leave me riling.

"Six inch maps"? I asked.
He shook his head smiling,
His glasses reflect his power
To leave me riling.

"Not any more" he said.
He cocked his head smiling,
"They are all metric now".
Still he left me riling.

"You know what I mean".
He shook his head half-smiling,
"No afraid not" he said
Leaving me riling.

"Of Bedfordshire" I said
Nodding my head smiling.
His glasses reflect my power
To leave him riling.

"In the Red Book" I said
I lean into his face smiling.
He sways away in his chair
I sense his riling.

"I'd like to see it"
I said, broadly smiling.
"Certainly sir" he said grimly
Trying to hide his riling.

"Is this it" he said
Dropping the book, not smiling.
"Yes, - but I've changed my mind",
"Put it back", I said "In the filing".

He stands there
No longer smug or smiling,
His glasses still perched on his nose
And I was no longer riling.

*****

THE RAIN

A billion drops of rain
Lie resting in placid pools
Doubling the landscape
And giving the sky a twin.
Their newly found unison
Responding only to gravity
And the mortifying wind
Fresh from the Gulags.

Vaporised by the sun
The pools rise mistily
And vanish slowly
Writhing in pain from
The slow transformation
According to laws written
In the distant genesis
Of the Big Bang.

St. Joseph's a Remembrance

1

In the name of all who were there
And lived to tell the tale
Those days of distant misery
Are washed with tears of time.

The anger and despair Billy
May be recalled at will
But days of distant memory
Are washed with tears of time.

In the fastness of your memory Joey
The fights you fought and lost
Over and over and over again
Are washed with tears of time.

They say things have changed Bernie
And we may grant it so but
You carry scars that still remain
Though washed with tears of time.

And all those pals you made Maurice
You've seen them come and go
Those days at Enfield unforgotten
Though washed with tears of time.

2

O Hallowed be thou name
Jimmy Langrell, Peter Crotty,
Lionel Essex, John Crawley,
From each a sacrifice cruelly drawn.

On his very first trip to Europe
Dropping bombs on folk unknown,
Jimmy navigating his Wellington
Met his personal Waterloo.

Peter Crotty lost his hand
And nobody ever found it.

Lionel in a foxhole on Hill 65
When the Chinese came on in a flood,
Lionel was a hero for a year and a day
And alone with his nightmares thereafter.

Johnny had a head of white curly hair
And cheeks that were permanently red,
But I was his friend and I didn't see
Lungs that were full of Tubercular thread

3

Of the numerous days in a decade,
Three thousand six hundred and more,
Perhaps only one hundred and fifty
Are recalled with a smile and a nod.

Yes they gave us our daily bread
And yes they forgave us our sins,
And yes they forgot all about love
And they found no time for respect.

So sing me no songs of times gone by
That were full of memorable joy,
If you were not there with us and alone
There's no way you could possibly know.

******

THE BROTHERHOOD

1. Early Days

The bond was forged in adversity
When our life was young,
Hardship and helplessness
Arrived with the morning sun
And persisted like endless rain.

Anger gave no respite
To daily injustice.
Nobody escaped its
Grinding pain.

Boys and nuns alike
Trapped by the pre-war
Mores of brutality,
Case-hardened and rendered
Blind to vulnerability.

Resilience was the saviour,
With it came survival.
But for some, deep scars
Left them unable to forget.

Bright sun amid the rain
Brought memorable rainbows.
Summer camp, trips to the park,
Games not known or played elsewhere,
Releasio, All the Ball, King,
Boots-Shoes-Tips or Nails,
Played with commitment
Forgetting daily hardship.

A regime of relentless pettiness
Kept us captive but unbowed.
Authority was king
Right or wrong,
Edible food not allowed.

To the friendship of peers
Subtract the bullyboys
Leaving the joys
Less than the tears.

Surviving without rancour
Was the price of entry
To phase one of a Brotherhood
That was to flourish
Three score years and more.

The year of release was notched
On many a memory stick
And the months counted down
To grow into years,
With the infinite patience
Of those who knew
Time was on their side.

2. The End

Leaving at last
We sense escape
But dare not say.
The gods are listening
And implacable.

Exultation stifled

The carriage doors close
Bringing finality
To a journey through darkness.
We peer through the window,

Regimentation dissolving

As St Joseph's slides away,
Sloughed off with the passing townscape.
Independence hovering
As the train rhythmically and relentlessly
Casts off the shackles
That bound us together for a decade
Of authoritarian misrule.

3. The Transition

On the train came the memory loss
Wiped clean by the pure joy of leaving,
To resurface in some aeon to come.
Now was the time
To eat our sandwiches,
Without permission.
Not minding our Ps,
Not minding our Qs.
Stand up, sit down.
Do as we please,
Look out of the window.
Can we? May we?
You bet!
Those people, can't they see?
Don't they feel?
We're dizzy with freedom.
O! everything is golden
We're going to explode
Into a thousand pieces
Each with the same lustrous message,
We're free! For God's sake we're free!
We will never go back
Wild horses and all the Kings men.

4. The Beginning

We arrived on a balmy evening
On a train at Blaisdon Halt,
When it left a few moments later
Around us the blackbirds were singing.

A blanket of tranquillity softly fell
Not known or experienced before,
As the train slowly vanished from view
Leaving Blaisdon to weave its own spell.

A man appeared in a cassock black
With hands in his pockets and smiling,
We picked up our parcels and followed
Not knowing we would never look back.

Like the Pied Piper he led us a dance
To the Hall in the woods on the hill
And chatted to us as though equal
While we looked at each other askance.

He introduced himself as a Brother
And we felt we had passed through a door
To a future that was suddenly brighter
That was now down to us and no other.

There followed two years of bliss
As we charted a course for our future
With the help of our brothers, the Salesians,
Feeling nothing could be better than this.

We now know those feelings were right,
Confirmed as the years quickly passed
That the bond that binds us to Blaisdon
Will last 'til that final Good Night.

5. Epilogue

The long years of harshness,
The sudden escape from grief,
Gave common cause that bound us
With a strength beyond belief.

The alchemy wrought by Blaisdon,
Salesians and their philosophy,
Brought us to a kingdom
Where ruled respect and fraternity.

******

A Visit to the Blaisdon Old Boys Grave

The Severn Vale lays open to the sky,
The church sits patiently on the hill,
Its bells are calling, calling
But from some there'll be no reply.

We talk together under an April sky,
The church waits patiently upon the hill,
Behind us the orchard is in bloom,
Our thoughts for friends and life's gone by.

Befriended by this hamlet long ago
From a common Dickensian horror,
We thought it paradise when we came
And have never ceased to think it so.

A sadness lightly lays itself around
The group of elderly men that stand
To pay respect for friends long gone
In silence rich without a sound.

We gather around the communal stone
And cast a prayer upon the breeze
And for a moment the group unites
With thoughts of friends no longer alone.

The Severn Vale is not aware,
The church has seen it all before,
But under the trees lays the stone
A reminder old friends will always care.

We shuffle and pause reluctant to return
To cars that will bear us on our way,
From this poignant and bucolic charm,
From Blaisdon for which we'll always yearn.

******

Nightfall

Behind the sloping oak
The sky looms with portent.
Fingers of cloud stretch menacingly;
A breeze escaping from the woods
Rattles the leaves of the leaning oak.

Soon the sun dies without hope
And the oak leaves burn black
In the embers of the dead sun.
The distant landscape hides in darkness;
The day is done.

We gather around the communal stone
And cast a prayer upon the breeze
And for a moment the group unites
With thoughts of friends no longer alone.

The Severn Vale is not aware,
The church has seen it all before,
But under the trees lays the stone
A reminder old friends will always care.

We shuffle and pause reluctant to return
To cars that will bear us on our way,
From this poignant and bucolic charm,
From Blaisdon for which we'll always yearn.

******

Nightfall

Behind the sloping oak
The sky looms with portent.
Fingers of cloud stretch menacingly;
A breeze escaping from the woods
Rattles the leaves of the leaning oak.

Soon the sun dies without hope
And the oak leaves burn black
In the embers of the dead sun.
The distant landscape hides in darkness;
The day is done.

NOTES

The intention of these notes is to shed a little light on how some of the poems came to be written rather than what they might mean. The latter is in the hands of you the reader. I have always been interested in the process of writing poetry and I am hopeful these notes will interest you. Not all poems are commented upon.

'Glimpses' One morning, sixty odd years ago, attending a service in the farm chapel I was wool gathering as usual when a train of thought led to me trying to visualize eternity. After some time concentrating hard I quite suddenly seemed to be carried into an understanding of eternity. It was gone almost as soon as it arrived and I was left, with the memory which, I was never able to conjure up again. This poem records the occasion sixty years later.

'Abandoned' A chance remark by a five year old niece when ushered into the ward to see the body of her mother, stayed with me on and off for many years.
Ten years later it seemed right to develop what was a very personal thought of a very young person.

'The River Runs Over My Bones' This phrase came uninvited into my head. I liked the sound of it but it was three or four months before I felt able to tackle it. The poem pretty well then wrote itself without much preamble. I found the imagery disturbing as it unfolded.

'Once Upon a Time' This was intended for my Grandchildren to make them aware of the direction we, on their behalf, were heading. The disaster movie ending shows how it got out of hand.

'On Marcle Ridge' Was written on the spot. My Daughter and I quite unexpectedly stumbled on the site. We sat on the memorial bench admiring the landscape and wondering about the family who had left such a simple and moving memorial. A poem seemed appropriate.

'Making a Call from Ireland' Recalls the difficulty I had trying to telephone my wife in the UK from a remote village in County Sligo.

The landlord of the pub where I was having lunch sold me a telephone card. I was assured it would make the process simple. Not so simple for me. I had to work hard on this poem having decided to base it upon the rhythm and approach of Henry Reed's 'The Naming of the Parts' from his 'Lessons of the War.'

'I Remember Charlie' Charlie was a farm labourer of a type that disappeared with the increase in mechanisation on mixed arable and dairy farms. Shabbily treated and unappreciated despite his skills, he was uncomplaining and undemanding. I knew him sixty years ago and the acceptance of his lot and especially his fear of the workhouse has stayed with me. It seemed to me someone should remember him.

'The Ploughing Team' Based upon my own experience it seeks to put on record the technical aspects as well as the rhythm that emerges between horses and ploughman. A friend suggested that the number of people with experience of ploughing with horses was not large and the experience should be recorded.

'Softly is the Hill' Turned out to be a nostalgic view of my experience of working the land with horses. The title phrase came first – unbidden – and the next three lines two or three weeks later. The next three verses suggested themselves six to eight weeks after that. Although related in feeling to "The Ploughing Team", this poem was written about two years later. A good example of a single phrase developing in a direction that was not foreseen at the outset; the mind, presumably, working quietly in the interim.

'The Stag' This was in part inspired by R.S.Thomas's 'The Gap in the Hedge.' From our kitchen window can be seen the remnants of an upright dead tree. With a little imagination it takes on the form of the proverbial *Stag at Bay.*
Whenever I looked it seemed always to be staring in my direction, head up and challenging. Eventually it encouraged me to imagine a head-to- head confrontation, the poem was the result.

'St. Joseph's a Remembrance' Written in an approximate paraphrase of the prayer known as 'Our Father', it touches on a grim period in my early life when attending a school in the 1930s and 1940s where there had been an incessant emphasis on prayer and abusive discipline Some lads then went off to the war and were dealt an especially cruel hand following as it did a grievous childhood. Written for them and my friends and enemies of that time.

'The Brotherhood' Is the tale of a grim start to life that I and many boys experienced in the years between the wars in an urban religious institution. It was followed by a transfer, for many, to a Salesian College in rural Gloucestershire. It was like a transfer from purgatory to Paradise. The experience, unknown to us who went through it, forged a bond that has remained with us seventy years later. The poem is written for, and dedicated to, members of the Brotherhood and describes elements of the journey